91.568 Gib
bons, Gail,
ration /
.99
098217860

HARRIS COUNTY PUBLIC LIBRARY

D1090581

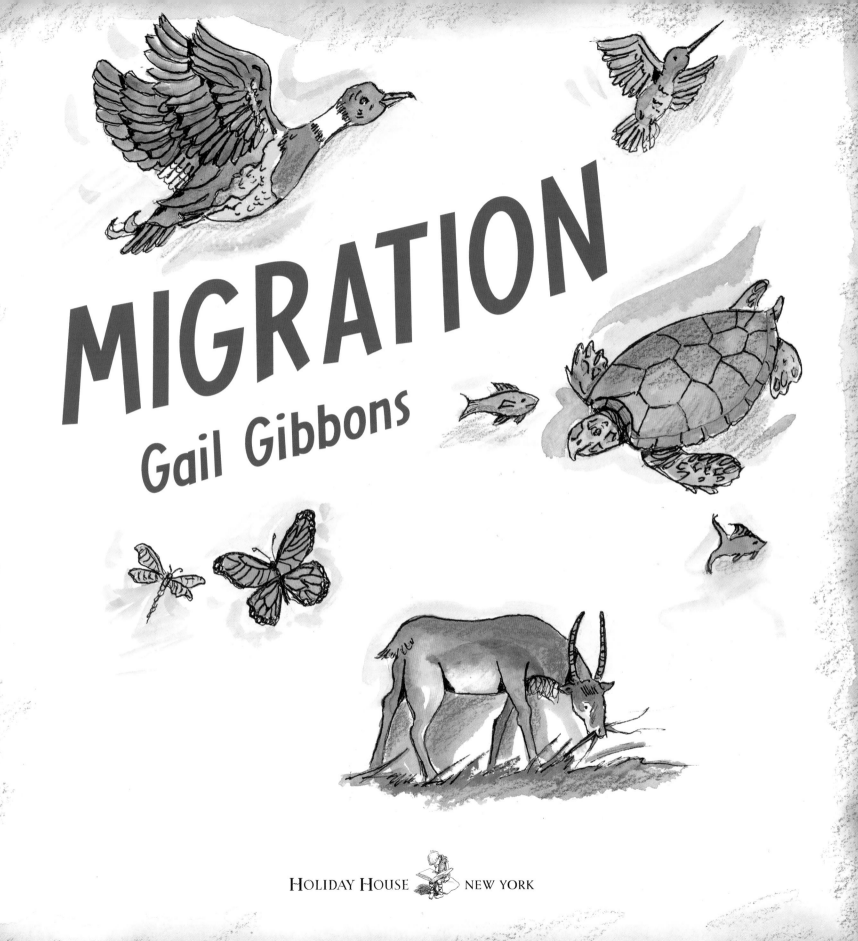

MIGRATION

Gail Gibbons

HOLIDAY HOUSE · NEW YORK

Special thanks to Jim Doherty, General Curator Emeritus of the New York Zoological Society, for his expert reading and consultation on this book.

Copyright © 2020 by Gail Gibbons
All Rights Reserved
HOLIDAY HOUSE is registered in the U.S. Patent and Trademark Office.
Printed and bound in March 2020 at Toppan Leefung, DongGuan City, China.
The artwork was created on watercolor paper with black ink, watercolors, and colored pencil.
www.holidayhouse.com
First Edition

Library of Congress Cataloging-in-Publication Data

Names: Gibbons, Gail, author.
Title: Migration / by Gail Gibbons.
Description: First edition. | New York : Holiday House, [2020] | Audience: Ages 4-8. | Audience: K to Grade 3.
Identifiers: LCCN 2019015803 | ISBN 9780823440658 (hardcover)
Subjects: LCSH: Animal migration—Juvenile literature.
Classification: LCC QL754 .G53 2020 | DDC 591.56/8—dc23
LC record available at https://lccn.loc.gov/2019015803

MIGRATION means to travel to a new environment that will better meet an animal's needs.

Let's get going! In the animal kingdom some creatures are becoming restless. They are beginning to feel the need to move. Migration is about to begin.

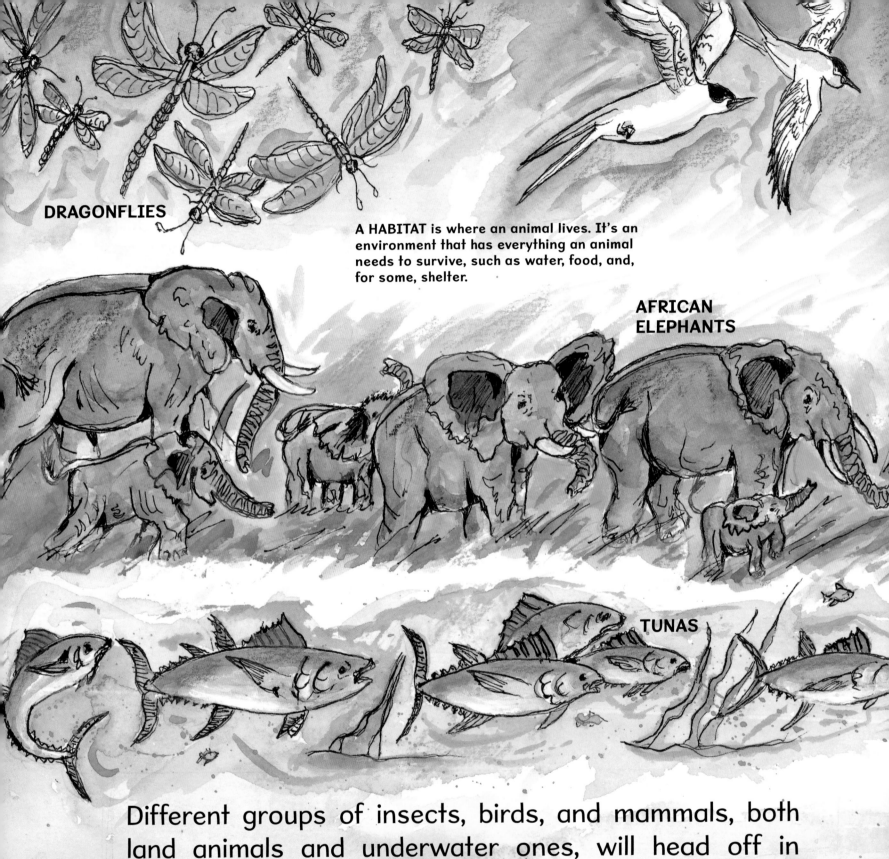

DRAGONFLIES

A HABITAT is where an animal lives. It's an environment that has everything an animal needs to survive, such as water, food, and, for some, shelter.

AFRICAN ELEPHANTS

TUNAS

Different groups of insects, birds, and mammals, both land animals and underwater ones, will head off in different directions. They will leave their habitats.

ARCTIC TERNS

LADYBUGS

CLIMATE is the normal weather in a region.

ADÉLIE PENGUINS

Animals migrate to try to reach climates that are better for them. Often animals move to mate and to raise their young in more suitable conditions.

PINK-SPOTTED HAWKMOTH

COMMON BLUE BUTTERFLY

ROBIN

RED ADMIRAL BUTTERFLY

GAZELLES

Earth

NORTH POLE

EQUATOR

SOUTH POLE

PINTAIL DUCKS

Back and forth these migrations go throughout the years according to seasonal changes. Each species knows what it needs to survive. An animal's needs depend on where on Earth it lives.

ARCTIC TERNS

POLAR BEARS

SOCKEYE
SALMON

Some animals will travel thousands of miles or kilometers
to their final destination. Others migrate short distances.

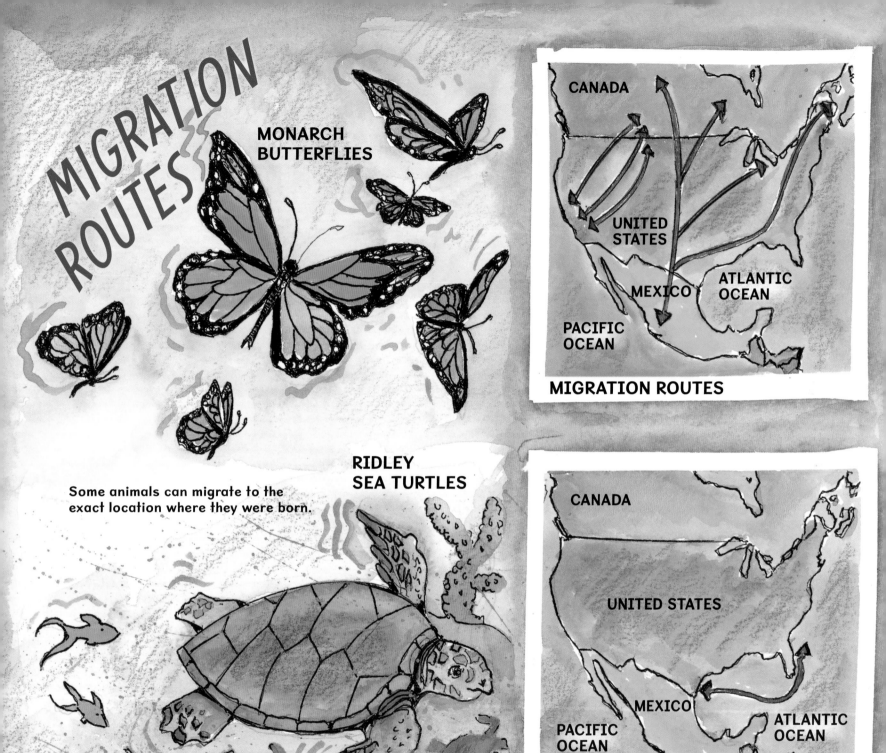

MIGRATION ROUTES

MONARCH BUTTERFLIES

MIGRATION ROUTES

Some animals can migrate to the exact location where they were born.

RIDLEY SEA TURTLES

MIGRATION ROUTES

Scientists and others try to understand how different animals know when to gather in groups to migrate.

Some migrators watch for landmarks.

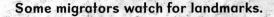

TUNDRA SWANS

Some navigate at night using the positions of the stars to guide them.

CANADA GEESE

Earth's Magnetic Field

Others notice seasonal changes caused by shifts in the sun's position in the sky. At different times of the year, the shifts make days become longer or shorter.

REINDEER

Some scientists believe the magnetic pull between the North and South Poles helps animals migrate. They believe the bodies of some animals contain a mineral called MAGNETITE (MAG-nuh-tight). The magnetite tells the animals which way is north or south.

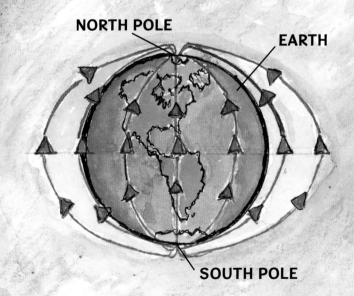

NORTH POLE

EARTH

SOUTH POLE

It's amazing how the migrators remember the exact routes to take year after year.

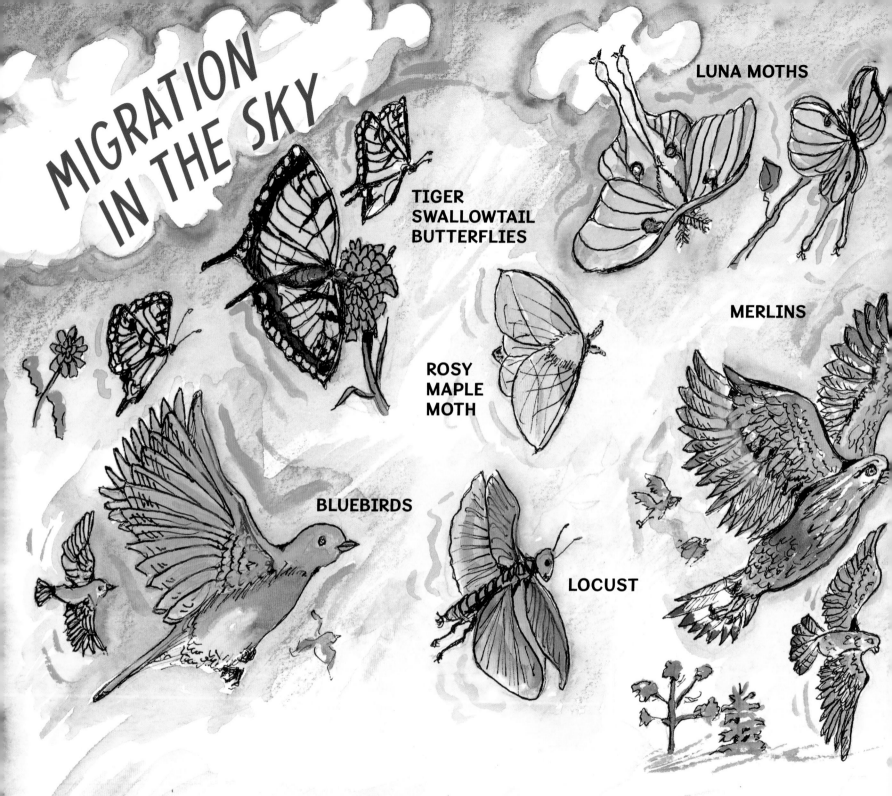

MIGRATION IN THE SKY

LUNA MOTHS

TIGER SWALLOWTAIL BUTTERFLIES

MERLINS

ROSY MAPLE MOTH

BLUEBIRDS

LOCUST

It's hard to believe that tiny, delicate insects can fly long distances. Birds do this, too. Insects and birds gather into groups of the same species to migrate.

HUMMINGBIRDS

WHOOPING
CRANES

BLUE
HERONS

Small and large birds fill the skies. Many birds point their heads in the direction they will travel to tell others in the group the way to go.

MALLARD DUCKS

MIGRATION ROUTES

ALASKA
CANADA
UNITED STATES
MEXICO
PACIFIC OCEAN
ATLANTIC OCEAN

MEXICAN FREE-TAILED BATS

MIGRATION ROUTES

NORTH AMERICA
ATLANTIC OCEAN
PACIFIC OCEAN
SOUTH AMERICA

Often birds and bats migrate at night. Mallard ducks use the North Star and the patterns of the stars to guide them.

CANADA GEESE

The ripples of air forming the V shape
are called an UPWASH.

MIGRATION ROUTES

ALASKA

CANADA

UNITED
STATES

PACIFIC
OCEAN

MEXICO

ATLANTIC
OCEAN

Canada geese fly in a V-shaped formation because it makes
flying easier. Ripples in the air from the V shape create an
air path so the geese don't have to flap their wings so hard.

SANDHILL CRANES

THERMAL AIR CURRENTS

Sandhill cranes fly very high in the sky into upper air currents. They soar on thermal winds so they don't need to flap their wings as much to fly.

ARCTIC TERNS

In 12 months they can fly 25,000 miles (over 40,000 km).

On their migrations they follow coastlines, diving to catch their food.

MIGRATION ROUTES **NORTH POLE**

GREENLAND

NORTH AMERICA

ATLANTIC OCEAN

EUROPE

ASIA

AFRICA

SOUTH AMERICA

INDIAN OCEAN

AUSTRALIA

PACIFIC OCEAN

ANTARCTICA

SOUTH POLE

Arctic terns migrate farther than any other animal! They can fly from the North Pole to the South Pole and back! They follow the sun's path to stay warm.

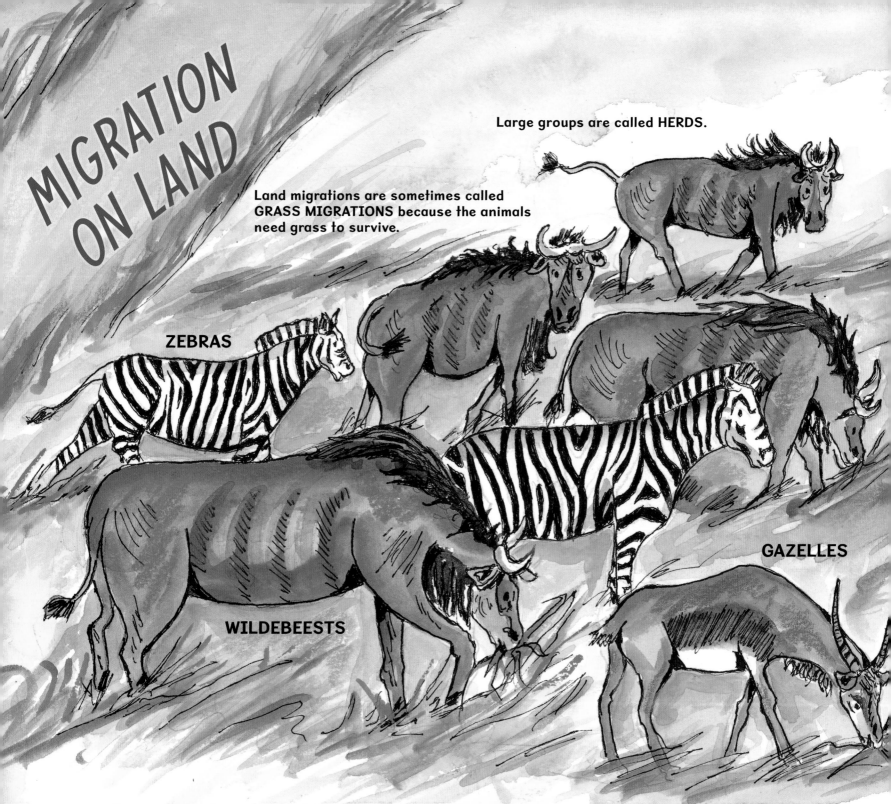

MIGRATION ON LAND

Large groups are called HERDS.

Land migrations are sometimes called GRASS MIGRATIONS because the animals need grass to survive.

ZEBRAS

WILDEBEESTS

GAZELLES

Land animals migrate to better climates in search of food and to mate and raise their young.

Some GAZELLES have hooves that give off scents for others to follow.

Africa

KENYA

TANZANIA

MIGRATION ROUTES

Often ZEBRAS, GAZELLES, and WILDEBEESTS migrate together.

In central Africa there are mass migrations of animals seeking fresh grass, water, and a better climate.

CARIBOU can migrate 1,000 miles (1,600 km).

CARIBOU

MIGRATION ROUTES

ATLANTIC OCEAN

ALASKA

CANADA

PACIFIC OCEAN

NORTH AMERICA

Caribou travel in huge herds. Some herds have more than 100,000 caribou! In the spring they migrate north.

ELEPHANTS usually travel in groups of up to 400. They surround their young to protect them as they move along.

ELEPHANTS

MIGRATION ROUTES

AFRICA

ATLANTIC OCEAN

Elephants live in herds and migrate. Usually they travel to areas where water holes have filled or formed from recent rains. This also means there will be more food.

MIGRATION ROUTES

NORWAY

FINLAND

REINDEER

MIGRATION ROUTES

RUSSIA

ALASKA

ARCTIC ICE CAP

CANADA

GREENLAND

HUDSON BAY

POLAR BEARS

Many animals migrate over land, looking for just the right climate.

MIGRATION IN THE WATER

The male keeps the egg warm under its tummy feathers. He carefully balances the egg on his front feet.

During this time the female is fishing out at sea.

A FEMALE EMPEROR PENGUIN lays only one egg.

In about two months, the chick is born.

When the chicks are strong enough, they join their parents at sea.

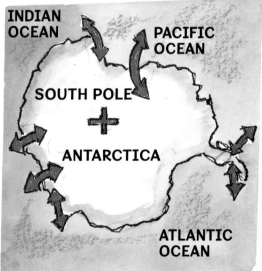

MIGRATION ROUTES

INDIAN OCEAN

PACIFIC OCEAN

SOUTH POLE

+

ANTARCTICA

ATLANTIC OCEAN

A lot of migration goes on underwater. Some birds actually migrate by swimming through ocean waters. In the winter Emperor penguins migrate to places where the ice is thick enough to support a large group gathering to have their young.

GREEN SEA TURTLE

LEATHERBACK SEA TURTLE

The warm sand INCUBATES the eggs to keep them warm.

After hatching, baby turtles hurry to get to the safety of the seawater.

The LEATHERBACK SEA TURTLE makes the longest turtle migration—about 9,000 miles (14,000 km).

GREEN SEA TURTLE MIGRATION ROUTES

NORTH AMERICA

SOUTH AMERICA

PACIFIC OCEAN

AUSTRALIA

Sea turtles spend their lives in the ocean. A few weeks after mating the female migrates to a beach to lay her eggs. Then she covers them with sand and hurries back to the ocean away from predators.

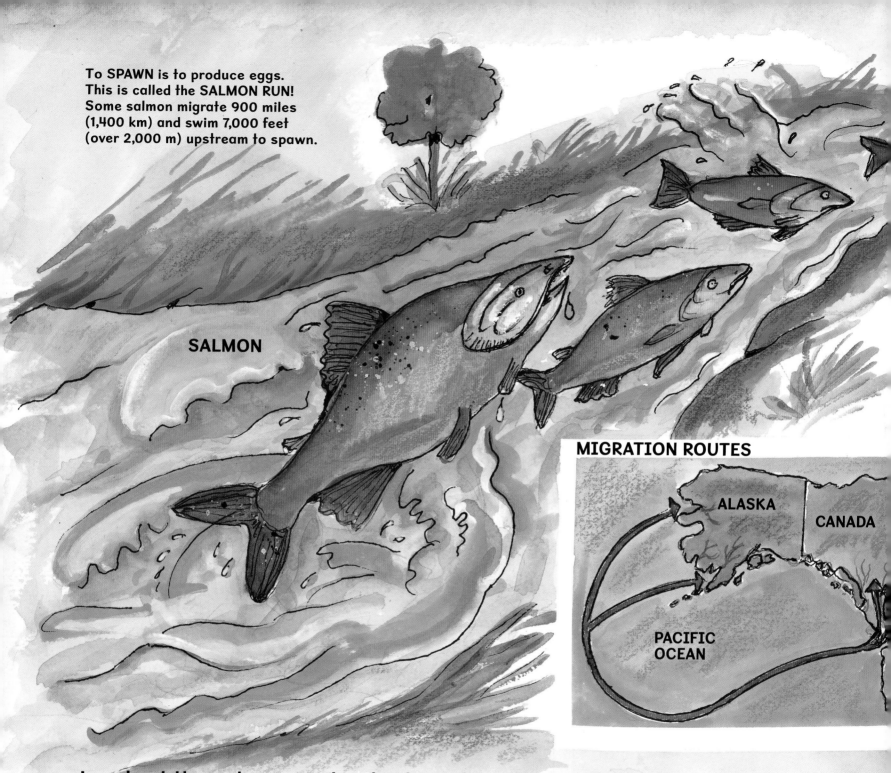

To SPAWN is to produce eggs. This is called the SALMON RUN! Some salmon migrate 900 miles (1,400 km) and swim 7,000 feet (over 2,000 m) upstream to spawn.

SALMON

MIGRATION ROUTES

ALASKA

CANADA

PACIFIC OCEAN

Look at them leap and splash! Salmon come from the ocean, fighting their way up rivers and streams as water rushes toward them. They are migrating to their spawning grounds to produce their young.

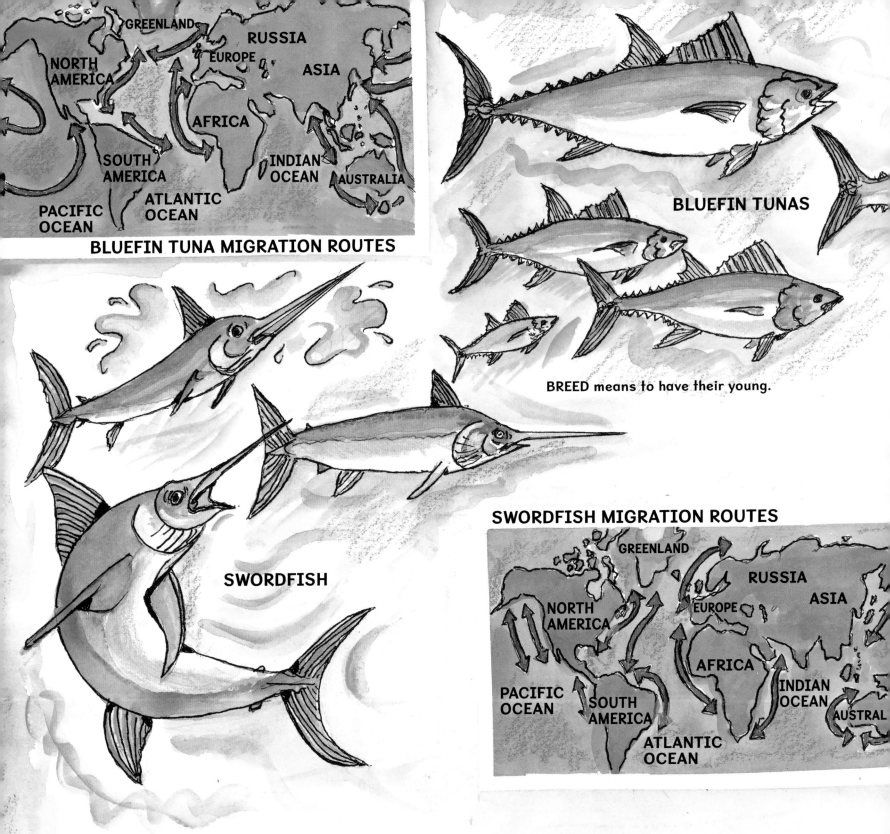

BLUEFIN TUNA MIGRATION ROUTES

BLUEFIN TUNAS

BREED means to have their young.

SWORDFISH

SWORDFISH MIGRATION ROUTES

Some tuna migrate to find better feeding areas or to breed.
Swordfish do this, too.

WALRUSES

RUSSIA

ARCTIC
OCEAN

NORTH
POLE

GREENLAND

ATLANTIC
OCEAN

PACIFIC
OCEAN

NORTH
AMERICA

MIGRATION ROUTES

Huge walruses live in the Arctic region. They migrate south in the fall to find foods such as snails and crabs. In the spring they migrate north to give birth and raise their young.

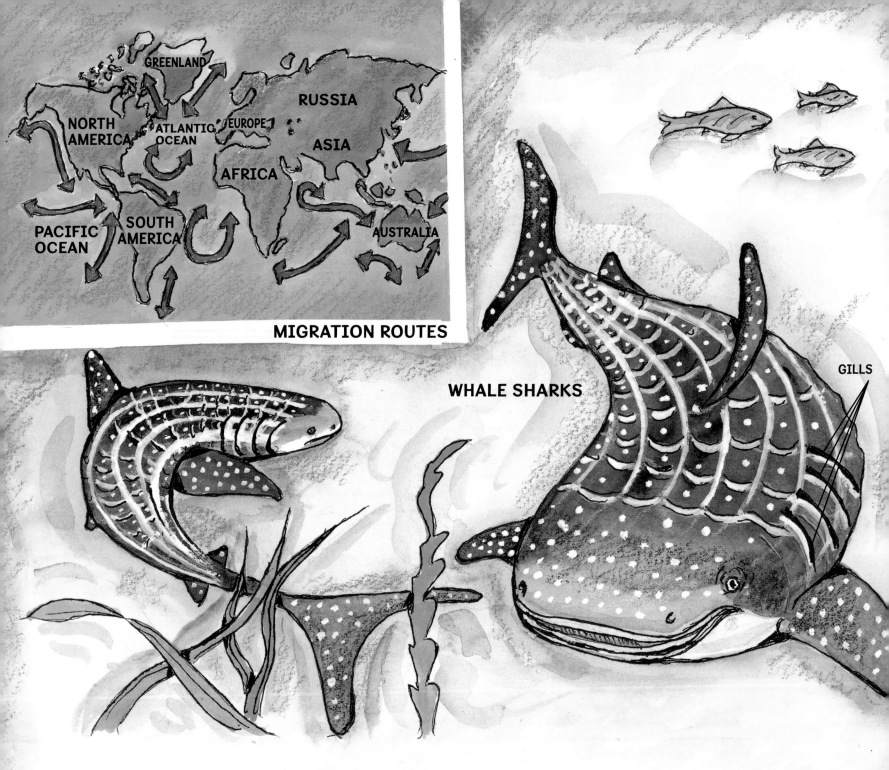

MIGRATION ROUTES

GREENLAND
RUSSIA
NORTH AMERICA
ATLANTIC OCEAN
EUROPE
ASIA
AFRICA
PACIFIC OCEAN
SOUTH AMERICA
AUSTRALIA

WHALE SHARKS

GILLS

Some sharks migrate, too. Whale sharks are the world's biggest fish. They migrate to the best feeding areas to find safe places to give birth to their young. They swim about 7,000 miles (about 11,000 km) a year.

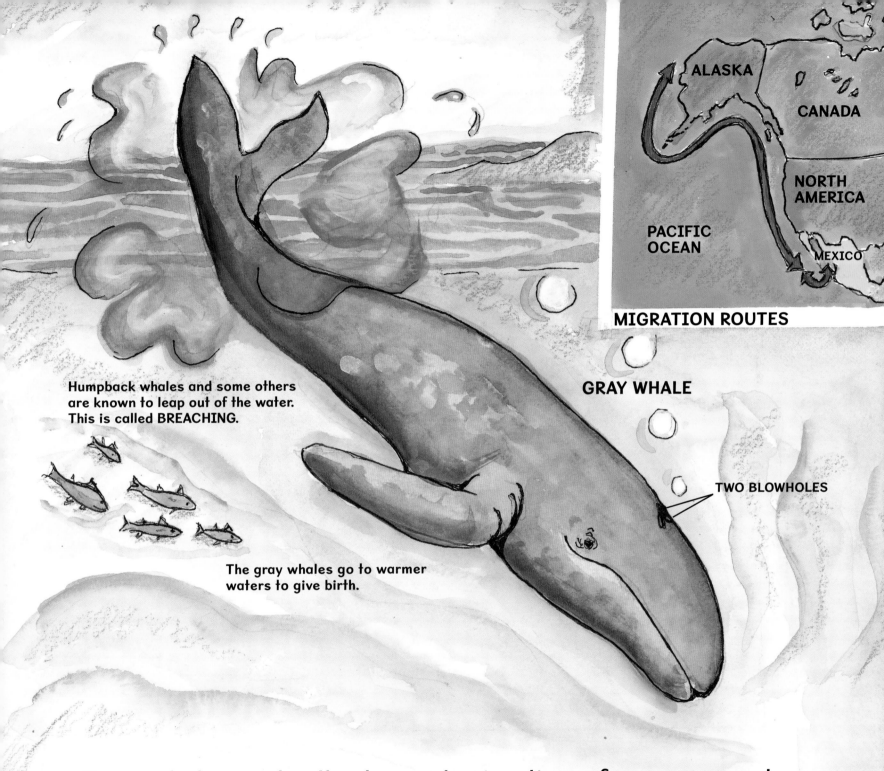

ALASKA

CANADA

NORTH AMERICA

PACIFIC OCEAN

MEXICO

MIGRATION ROUTES

GRAY WHALE

TWO BLOWHOLES

Humpback whales and some others are known to leap out of the water. This is called BREACHING.

The gray whales go to warmer waters to give birth.

Gray whales make the longest migration of any mammal. They swim up to 12,000 miles (nearly 20,000 km) during their journey. Because they are mammals, whales need air. They must surface to breathe oxygen through their blowholes.

BLUE WHALE

The biggest whale of all is the blue whale. It is the largest creature that has ever lived. It can be 100 feet long (about 30 meters) and weigh 180 tons.

MIGRATION ROUTES

NORTH AMERICA

GREENLAND

RUSSIA

EUROPE

ASIA

PACIFIC OCEAN

AFRICA

PACIFIC OCEAN

SOUTH AMERICA

ATLANTIC OCEAN

INDIAN OCEAN

AUSTRALIA

Every one to three years the BLUE WHALE swims about 9,500 miles (about 15,000 km).

These whales migrate to warmer waters to breed.

People enjoy watching insects, butterflies, and birds flutter and fly as they migrate to their new climates.

Some people go to zoos where they learn about the migrators. Others go on whale watches. Back and forth, year after year, migrations keep animals on the go.

LET'S GET GOING

Many animals have adapted to their climate and survive in all seasons.

COTTONTAIL RABBIT

BROWN BEAR

Some animals HIBERNATE, meaning they sleep motionless in winter in protected places until their climate warms up.

WILDEBEEST

ZEBRA

ARCTIC TERN

An Arctic tern, because of its long migrations, could travel about 60 times around Earth during a lifetime.

Zebras, wildebeests, and other wildlife in Africa migrate clockwise in a giant circle. Their search for water and food takes them through the rainy periods as the seasons change.

Emperor penguins walk about 125 miles (about 200 km) over ice to their nesting grounds.

EMPEROR PENGUINS

FROG

Some reptiles and amphibians have short migrations to deposit their eggs in or close to the nearest body of water.

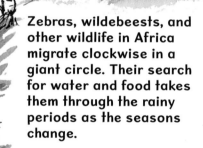

Some people help feed migratory animals by growing plants such as wildflowers that they need to survive.

EGGS

Some people help salmon by building SALMON LADDERS that the fish use to go upstream.

WHALE

Because of global warming, some sea creatures are migrating closer to the poles, where the seawater is colder.